Für die Liebe.

Für das Leben.

J.M.

Through The Eyes Of A Heart

.

J. M.

Through The Eyes Of A Heart

poems

Impressum

Bibliografische Information der Deutschen Nationalbibliothek:
Die Deutsche Nationalbibliothek verzeichnet diese Publikation in der Deutschen Nationalbibliografie; detaillierte bibliografische Daten sind im Internet über http://dnb.dnb.de abrufbar.

Lektorat: Julia Mertins
Umschlaggestaltung & Layout: Julia Mertins

Herstellung und Verlag: BoD – Books on Demand, Norderstedt

ISBN: 978-3-7578-0268-4

Table of content

FALL FOR YOU

I want to fall for you
Over
And
Over
Again.
Like you fall for me.
Every year.
You awaken that longing in me.
Longing for warmth.
Longing for silence.
Longing for security.
You make ma wanna fall for you.
Over. And. Over. Again.
You don't seem to have a glimpse
Of how badly I'm awaiting you.
Every year.
Still, you come back.
Every year.
To shine for me in all your colors.
So simple.
Yet so beautiful.

You fill me up with love.
I'm breathing you in.
I'm breathing you in.
You're silent giant.
Destructive and simple.
And you're not just there.
You arrive quietly.
Still, it seems like you come suddenly.

One day, each year, you arrive.
And it seems like you say
„Hey, it's me again. It's been a year."
You don't ask questions.
But you want to hear mine.
And you don't have quite the answers I'm looking for.
Yet, you always seem to respond.
When I close my eyes, I can hear you whisper.
Softly, calming, caring.

And I'm falling for you.
Like you fall for me.
Every year.
Over and over again.

BEHOLD, BE BOLD

The want to arrive, the need to let go.
The longing for security, the longing for freedom.

Always looking.
Never resting.
Always searching.
Never resting.
Always on the run.
Never resting.
Never resting.

Is this right?
No. But is it wrong?
Also no. What is it?
What is this?
What is all of this?
And why? Why.

Always questioning,
Wondering,
Wandering,
Forming,
Doubting,
Responding,
Depending,
Spending.

Incredibly fast, incredibly easy.
Everything is so easy, if you close your eyes.

You need to do it.
You need to stop it.
You need to start.
You need to keep going.
You need to need.
You need to now.

Never rest, never stay.
Never underestimate.
Overpower, out of fuel.
You need to work,
This gem, that jewel.
You need to carve, create and care.
One second here, then anywhere.

Save, crave behave.
Manners, minds, maneuvers.

You need to breathe.
You need to breathe.
You
Need
To
Breathe.

Then start again.
And start right there.
And keep your eyes
On what to share.
You need to be.
And become.
And be aware.
And be strong.

And always keep going.

And keep your mind on track.
And your heart on time.
And your thoughts focused.
And your passion, oh child.
You need to keep your passion.
And yourself together.

You will arrive.
You will let go.
You will share tears.
You can turn your back.
Don't turn your heart.
Never turn the heart.
Never.
Turn the heart.

Wrap yourself around it.
It's worth it.
And you will arrive.

If you keep going,
You will start going strong.
Not right then, but then some time.

Don't move too fast, enjoy what's there.
Don't move too slow.
Embrace and share.

And breathe, my child, breathe in and out.
In with the power, out with the doubt.

Be patient, and strong, and kind.
And aware.
Then arrive.

Have security. Have freedom.
Have longing and a thirst.
And have what calms it.
And have what keeps it.
Be balanced.
Keep fighting, keep moving.

Then rest.

And rest.
And rest with passion.
And rest with love.
Embrace this rest.
And embrace the rest.

Then move again.
And move with passion.
And move with love.
And be kind, my child, be kind.
And soon, I promise.
Soon you will arrive.
And soon you will be home.
You will be home.

ICE WATER, SALT WATER

I

Lost at sea
In a boat that is
small enough for me
to feel lonely
big enough for me
to get lost in.
I'm sorry
I'm not sorry
I hit that iceberg
that made you fall off.
I'm sorry to not be able to be the one to give you wings
that you can actually fly with.
I'm not sorry I'm not sorry
that the wings I need are not made of your affection;
that the water you pour into my glass
isn't the water that stills my thirst;
that whatever you bring is not enough for me;

ICE WATER, SALT WATER

II

I'm sorry that in fact I'm afraid to be the one who woulnd't be
enough for you.
I'm sorry I didn't want to find out the hard way.
I'm sorry to let you find out the hard way.
The way that ice was involved with.
I didn't mean for that to happen.
As much as it was that's exactly as much as it wasn't
an accident or coincidence
to crash into that cold thing that is impossible to be handled.
I don't like hitting people
and I hit you hard
the way we met
the way we parted.
It's not fair for us to deal with
what we never asked for,
yet we decided to go on that trip together

ICE WATER, SALT WATER

III

And I decided to let you into that boat
that is too small to fit all of the boxes that tell my story;
Too small to carry the both of us.
Regardless of how much I wished for that to be possible.
I'm sorry the room I made was beyond my limits and
beyond everything I'm willing to share;
yet not the kind of room you need
to feel comfortably warm in
I'm sorry my tools were too frozen to warm us up.
I'm sorry my boat is so small that it only fits me perfectly,
and that everyone else to be on it
should bring a life boat
in case the waves get too big
in case the ice gets too cold for us to stand through
Together.

ALWAYS, LOVE

I will reach out to you, always
and will be here for
when you want to get rid of words
or thoughts
or whatever is going on with you.
I won't stop fishing for you, ever.

You just keep breathing, alright?
Keep breathing, so you'll keep your magic alive, love.

JUST

I want to sit on your lap
And have your head on my chest
And just hold you.
Close my eyes
And hear you breathe
And just hold you.
Softly stroke your neck with my fingers
Rest my cheek on your hair
And just hold you.

COTTONCANDY

Life is
like a
rollercoaster.

And while everyone
is standing
in line
to get the kick out of
ups and downs,

You're just somehow lost somewhere
trying to find
the ticket box

while eating
cotton candy
for the fifth time
today.

AGAINST SOME ODDS

Out of sight
Out of mind
yet in my heart
you will remain.

You left me there
Longing for you.
Now you're longing for me
And I'm longing for truth.

BURN IN A GOOD WAY

Work with you matches.
Start your fire.
Look for the light in your life.
Feed your fire.
Keep yourself alive.
Keep the fire alive.
As long as I care about that flame
The fire won't leave me.
As long as I do it will stay.

Let's take time to care about that light.
As long as we do
We will burn in a good way.

IMPATIENCE

How often
Do I stand there
And see this door close.

How much longer
Will I be wondering
Which door
Is about to open itself.

COLDISH WARM WITH A HINT OF BITTERSWEETNESS

It's autumn in my soul.
It's almost summer here.
But my soul feels like autumn.
It feels ready to snuggle up in that
warmish sweater,
with a cup of hot chocolate warming
the palms of my hands
while listening to the music
that is not christmas music,
But yet you can hear the sound of the bells
quite clear in the rough distance.
I'm ready for fall again.
Not ready to fall again.
Yet here I am.
Falling for summer in my soul.

COCOON

Spending time with you
Makes me wanna crawl back
Into my cocoon.

The things you say
Are the bricks of
The walls I'm building
Against you.

The way I am with you
Is beautiful.
It's like being a butterfly
Fully hatched.

Yet, you make me wanna go back
And develop more of myself.

More than I'm willing to show you
Or share with you.

B E Y O N D   W O R D S

Being beyond words to describe
a feeling.
Is being beyond my comfort zone
Yet more comfortable than I could have ever imagined.

Being beyond words to describe a feeling
Is being trapped in this very emotion
With no way other than
To feel it out.

Being beyond words to describe a feeling
Is creepy, and new, and embraceworthy,
And exciting, and unsure, and unknown.
And it makes my curiosity grow
And my heart even more.

Maybe being beyond words to describe a feeling
Is another, a new, a different way
To find peace
and find healing.

Being beyond words
Makes me shaky
And goofy
And quiet
And lost in thoughts
And trapped in actions
And forces me to reflect
Harder than I'd force myself.

Being beyond words
Makes me discover new ways
About myself
Of dealing with things.

Being beyond words
Is a complete disrupting, truthful, hurting, and healing,
A simple, and intense, and beautiful way
Of getting to know myself better.

DIVING DEEP IN UNKNOWN WATER

It's floating
And flying
And singing
And smiling.
And when the wave crashes
You're the one to find out
How beautiful deep diving can be.

So dive
And dive deeper
And let the water be the only thing
To hold you.

1 0 , 2 0 , 3 0

If there's one thing
that is important in this world
it's that time doesn't matter.

If you're looking at the circumstances
and what they bring to you
right now,
keep in mind how much they will matter
and not matter
within 10, 20, 30
days, weeks, years
from now.

A HEART

A heart that is
Bursting of joy
With every blink of the eye.

A heart that is
Full and can't be full enough
And has to be filled
More and more.

A heart that is
Calm, so calm.
So calm, when it's at the right place.
So calm and quiet.
And full of love
To be spread
To the right place

BROWN AND BLUE

I'm gonna wait
Where the sky is dark blue
And changes it's behavior by the minute.

I'm gonna wait
At the shoreline that is covered in the thoughts of both
My past and my future.

I'm gonna wait
Where blowing wind
Reminds me of your
And where peace is brought to my soul.

SUNRISE

I'm in a long distance relationship with the sunrise.
Every single moment we spend together is magic itself
and I always wish for it
to never end.
And when it's gone
it's another day;
like every other.
And I start hoping for the next day.
To see the sun rise again.

HOLE-HEARTED GOODBYE

I hate these
last days somewhere.
Those few
heart-beat-infused hours
before leaving a place.
Not knowing
When to expect yourself to be back.
And while your body is leaving the place
Your heart is leaving the body
and leaving a gap
to stay.

BAREFOOT IN SUMMER

Walking in sand
Is like walking through snow
But in summer.

Watching the sun set
Is like watching th leaves turn red
But in summer.

Watching the stars sparkle
Is like watching the flowers shyly grow
But in summer.

Watching the first shooting star
Is like a drop of water
When all you want is an ocean of what you can barely be
Bold enough to wish for.
But in summer.

BREATHE IN

I want to scream at the top of my
Long
Gone
Are we – and
have we been.
Ever since the day we first met.

I want to scream at the top of
my lungs
are filled with everything
too poisonous
for any person to breathe in.

Yet it gives me all the energy
to start over
now
Chapter 0.

YOU DO YOU; AND I ME

You lost me
when you chose to
search comfort in
the insecurity
and irritation
of another person.

You lost me
before I knew you did.
And as a consequence
that I'll have to carry responsibility for
forever
I choose to be
another person.
Another person
that's not a platform for your
insecurity and anger.

TAKE OUT FOR TWO

My hands are tied
up,
my thoughts are wrapped
up
and stored in one of the darker corners
of my mind,
right next to the other secrets I'm keeping
and supposed to keep, cause
naming them and giving them names
is giving you an idea
of how to deal and
if to deal with me.
I'll keep those closed up boxes
where they can't be reached.
Until someone's knife is soft enough not to cut
through heartstrings and
sharp enough to break down the boxes into
portions to consume
little by little
when shared.

FOREVER IS ONLY A WORD TO DESCRIBE SOMETHING IM TOO AFRAID OF FACING

Having you in her quiet thoughts annoyingly often was like having a blanket covering her restless, sweaty body for the dark, sweet, painfully hot nights in a summer she coulnd't imagine having before she lived through it:

Surprisingly necessary, and disgustingly hot, a little creepy even, and first and foremost calming;

knowing there's something that only lives to touch her in the moment she didn't even want to touch herself;

that stays to surround her, even when she's pushing it away, and staying furthermore even stronger and closer when after painfully distancing, almost surgically removing, as the blanket had become part of her body by melting into her, she wraps herself back into it completely.

To feel the security through every single pore and feel the heat fo up and up, never enough, since it's the only kind of heat no fever could reach, but the only thing mighty enough to cool down the race and sparkles and energy her thoughts are misusing to fuel the wrong engine.

WILD THOUGHTS

Drowning.
„Don't wait" by Mapei is ringing in the back of my head.
My neck hurts from headbanging last night.
Last night, when I had no wild thoughts.
Last night.
When I reached to my chest,
then to yours, then to yours.
Back to mine.
I reached my chest.
I held my hand on my heart.
I had to leave it there.
Too strong the vibrations.
Too certain the beat.
Too clear the fear.
The fear that this joy will be gone too soon.
I wanted to capture it.

Pure joy, exploding in my heart.
I don't know if it was the music or my heart.
Vividly blurred.
One with the music.
Never before have I felt so alive.
Surrounded mostly by strangers.
You smile, yelling, I don't understand,
I smile.
You hold my face with both your hands.
You shouldn't.
We yell, we don't understand.

Just music.
Too loud, but never loud enough
To make the thoughts stop –
Never loud enough.

Now my heart beats in silence.
But strong.
Too strong for the silence.
I wish I could put it on mute.
My stomach feels sick.
It usually doesn't.
Worries me.

You don't talk to me the way we used to talk.
No worries, you say.
You don't say much more.
I worry, you know?
You know.

„If it wasn't for you, I'd be alone"
It sounds like this other artist, you say.
To me it sounds much more like you for me.
You don't hear it.
Maybe your heart beats too loud for you to hear.
Maybe you have to get back to your main quest.
Maybe this is what I fear.
The fear that my joy will be gone too soon.
The fear of losing you.
I'm not ready for that.
I will never be ready for it.

Wild thoughts.
Running in my mind.
Without a rest,
Without a pause.

So many things to keep track of.
I'm drowing, my neck is killing me.
My throat as well.
I can't afford to be sick now.
I might be already.

The pen falls out of my hand.
It's time to sleep.
Let go of the thoughts.
Embrace the silence.
Sweat it out.
Sleep it out.

The joy you produce will stay with you,
No matter who is there to enjoy it with you.
The joy will never go away.
You don't have to hold it in your chest.

Free it. Share it. Double it.
Your eyes are tired.
Let the tiredness overflow your brain.
Don't fight it.
Keep fighting the good fight.
Embrace the silence.
And rest.
Tomorrow will be a new day.

BITTERSWEET WITH A HINT OF RAIN

I wish for you
To look at me
The way
That makes me say
„Break me"
For me
To feel whole again.

I wish for me
To suffocate
Within my own drought.
That's the water
My soul needs.

RAINY RUN AND SWEATY THOUGHTS

The summer heat has been going on for quite a while now.
The heat has been pushing down
On every body
Into every pore.

It's been getting worse when they started to announce the
rain for today.
Then for the next day,
then for the next day.
And now „today" is almost a week ago,
and it still hasn't been raining.

Today has been the today I have been waiting for all week.
I heard the first drop of water knocking on my window
like a long lost childhood friend
asking me if I wanted to come out and play until it gets dark.
I jumped up
And ran outside.
And I ran.
And I ran.
And I ran.
And I felt you getting off my mind.
I didn't know you were on there.
I felt you getting off my mind and out of my brain.
And my head started to hurt,
But that's what happens, when you miss something:
It hurts.
First it hurts your heart and at some point,
it goes to your head. And that hurts.
And while you start forgetting,

It hurts.
Luckily the headache will remind you of how ungrateful you
were
When your head didn't hurt.
So you run, to go forward.

The rain wasn't rushing.
It felt more like there was an event
And the main
„break the summer, give me something refreshing instead of
burning me smiling and make lose my mind" rain show act
didn't show,
So the back up rain had to,
And that rain is a bitter one.
It has you hoping for thunder and lightning
And cool, fresh air
That smell of the childhood everyone somehow remembers,
Although we don't spend that much time outside anymore,
When it's raining.
 - as if it was uninvited, but forced to come, and now it has
joined to do its part and leave as soon as possible –

And while that rain slowly stumbles upon everything
while it sprinkles on everything around you
And yourself.
You turn your body around
And start running backwards.

The rain slowly stops, while the heat,
that never really left,
settles back in.
And the sweat from today and last weeks today
And the tears from back then

And the rain from just now
They mix
And you,
While you run backwards away from what you're leaving
behind,
Smile and think about how easy it is
To run in the right direction,
Even when you're not seeing where you're heading.

It's so easy to run in the right direction blindly
when you see how fast the wrong things get smaller.

And you know you're ready for the main rain.

A PRAYER

Good Lord,
I pray for peace and serenity for my troubled state of mind.
I pray for compassion and patience
towards my peers impatience
with me and themselves.
I pray for You to open up our hearts
So we'll wake up and realize
what really matters.
I pray for You to never leave me
and for me to never want to leave you

Amen.

< N O T I T L E >

Two broken souls
To care for one another
Makes a thousand little flying needles
And one weak butterfly
To survive them all.

OVERFLOW AND BE OVERFLOWN

Don't be shy to love people, it happens
more often than you think.
Be shy with overflowing kindness to those
who don't respond to your love in love,
Always try and be kind.
Don't lie to yourself about your feelings.
Let your heart be filled by those who do love you.
Overflow and be overflown.
Give and receive.
Reload your heart with the energy you get
from loving and being loved.
Keep your heart full at all times.

EVENTUALLY

Choosing to wanting to be with you was simple,
cause the pain I'm imagining having
if I don't have you
is greater than the pain
I'm imagining having in case you
decide to leave some day.
And that's hard.

THE WALL IS YOUR FRIEND, BUT
EVERY WALL NEEDS A DOOR TO
LET IN THE PEOPLE WHO WILL
GIVE THEIR EVERYTHING TO
SUPPORT THE WALL FROM THE
SIDE YOU NEED THEM ON

Telling you that I'm not ready for your drama was the truth
once.
Realizing now I'm not ready for my own drama
is the truth
and has always been.
All that's left is hope.
Hope for the strength of that wall
to be turned into the energy I need
to go and face
what I've been hiding from behind the wall
for the longest time now.
Hope for this bond to never break the way I fear the most.
Hope.
That building this wall was only in self defense, and self care,
and seeking myself
and not
hiding away, and getting lost, and turning my head
from what is really important.

THE MAIN SIDE QUEST

When I tell others
about the way
you look at me,
Everyone tells me
you are the one.

The way you wait
for me to look into your eyes
So you know
That I'll hear
What you're about to say.
The way you let your glasses
slightly shift off your nose
Only to stare at me
Only to make me smile and look away quickly.
I don't blush often, but that's when I do.
Everyone tells me I'm crazy
I might be.
You're the one. You know it.
You're not the one-one.
You know it. I know it.
Nothing else matters.

R A I N

Did you ever have rain
drizzling down on your face?

Did you ever have rain
drizzling down on your face?

Face it.
Hold your face in it.
Have faith in it.

Did you ever have rain
drizzling down on your face?

TEARY RAIN AND RAINY TEARS

Tears rolling down your face
That's like rain rolling down your face.
Just natural.
More than natural
Yet
As naturally
As tears might come.

LET'S GRAB A COFFEE

In all the years
I've been participating
I have learned a thousand things.
I've never learned though
what it means to
Grab some coffee some time.

STORM WITHIN MYSELF

You were the storm
my restless heart needed
To be reminded of the peace
I can have
without you.

THIS CAKE IS A REAL PIECE OF WORK

You see a cake, a wonderful cake.
It's beautiful,
Beyond everything cake like
you've seen before.
But instead of saving it
you choose to cut into it.
Over and over again.
And you keep cutting
And you eat it all.
Until it's gone.
Gone for good.
Not for your good, though.
This cake may give you the worst stomach ache
You've ever experienced.

SNOWLESS MAGIC

The neighborhood is still as a silent winter morning just
when the first snow fell.
The snow is missing,
Though the wind is blasting so strong,
You wrap yourself up into your coat
twice as solid as you used to do.
Wind like the holy spirit,
Strong, stern, powerful, and soothing
To the soul that hasn't had enough
rest for a Tuesday morning,
When the neighborhood is still as a silent winter morning.
Just when the first snow fell.

THOUGHTS OF A DARK WEEK IN THE LIGHTS OF A SUNDAY, 10. JUNI '18

Yesterday I realized again how important it is to slow down life
And sit down on the patio in the sweet sunlight
listening to music directed straight to your ear
through the tiny speakers brought to you by technology.
I sat there, getting lost in the beauty of the moment,
that was so breathtaking, I was hesitant to pick up my phone,
because I was frightened for that to destroy this memory being built.
I asked myself how I was able to not really straight up listen to music
for about 6 months and how I had survived.

Within the past 2 weeks I went through some ups and more downs,
and I kept praying for me to keep going.
I prayed for strength and compassion and patience.
When love is delivered to you just like that, in the purest and most unconditional way,
and you can't respond in love, because you don't feel it,
you'll look for the reason within yourself
and you'll look – and most likely find – reasons to blame yourself
and maybe get lost in circles of thoughts that bring you down,
just because you forget that there's a sensible reason for your inability to love right back.
It's not you, darling, your heart is not broken, you're doing just fine.

Give it some time, and rest, and music and you will see the right path again.

The possibility of clouds and rain and thunderstorms on your path of life is omnipresent.

Don't forget that the path is there still, untouched by the storms and soaked by water to refresh your tired feet.

I had told myself to go to church again some time,
because that always gives me good feelings.

For a couple of months of going to church regularly it even felt like no matter

what struggle I'm going through or what thoughts keep being on my mind

the service is always about this very topic.

Let's say I'm moaning the death of a loved one – the service will give me input as to how to deal with the loss.

Or I kept having doubts about being a christian and been avoiding church and any contact with spiritual input and I decide to go back to church one day – finding Christ is the topic in this very service of me „coming back".

Or I kept being busy with life and trying to fit everything into the few 24 hours I have per day – church is giving me some kind of solution as to how to deal with time management regarding „god-things".

Today I went to church not knowing what I was looking for.
I haven't been last week.

The week before that I had the first talk to the pastor who was very inviting and uplifting in his choice of words for my ever so restless situation.

When I entered, the heat wave came upon me and I struggled to stay as to how it was about 3000 degrees in there.

Usually service opens with a song, today it opened with a
song and we kept singing.
Then we were introduced into how this would be a service of
praise, so just songs being sung.

Basically an invitation
to get lost within God
and be found within God.
To sing your heart and your pain and your prayer out
Or to sit or stand in silence
Eyes wide open or closed up still
And be moved by the music, and the lyrics and the spirit.
Exactly what I had discovered yesterday and planned on
doing more often within the near future.

I don't have words for how this affects me and what I'm
planning on doing with it.
Throughout the service I was reminded of both beautiful and
hurtful things.
And I couldn't help but sing and smile and sing and cry and
do all of it at the same time.
I just know that deep down in my heart
faith will always be of importance for the sanity of my soul
for the humbleness of my heart
and for the strength to keep going through whatever fog and
burning sun
I will have to go through,
because I know, no matter how lonely I will feel.
I will never be alone.

I DON'T KNOW, ARE YOU?

Are you done saving the world yet?
Are you done making everything about everyone besides
yourself yet?
Are you ready for that future you've been trying to build up
for the past year, two years, five years?
For the past forever?
You don't have answers, but you keep asking questions.
Stop the doubting.
But empower.
If the focus is right, the picture will clear and become
completely unblurry.
If you're facing the direction of travel, you'll have a better
view of when to stop and exit that bus.
Are you done saving the world yet?
Are you done, to save yourself?